North America

A Buddy Book
by
Cheryl Striveildi

ABDO
Publishing Company

VISIT US AT
www.abdopub.com

Published by Buddy Books, an imprint of ABDO Publishing Company, 4940 Viking Drive, Edina, Minnesota 55435. Copyright © 2003 by Abdo Consulting Group, Inc. International copyrights reserved in all countries. No part of this book may be reproduced in any form without written permission from the publisher.

Printed in the United States.

Edited by: Christy DeVillier
Contributing Editors: Matt Ray, Michael P. Goecke
Graphic Design: M. Hosley
Image Research: Deborah Coldiron
Photographs: Corbis, Corel, Eyewire, Getty Images, Minden Pictures, Photodisc

Library of Congress Cataloging-in-Publication Data

Striveildi, Cheryl, 1971-
    Continents. North America / Cheryl Striveildi.
        p. cm.
    Includes index.
    Summary: A brief introduction to the geography and various regions of North America.
    ISBN 1-57765-963-5
        1. North America—Juvenile literature. [1. North America.] I. Title: North America. II. Title.

E38.5 .S77 2003
917—dc21

                                                                    2002074660

Table of Contents

Seven Continents

Water covers most of the earth. Land covers the rest. The earth has seven main land areas, or continents. The seven continents are:

 North America

 Africa

 South America

 Asia

 Europe

 Australia

 Antarctica

North America is
a beautiful continent.

North America is the third-largest continent. Its land covers about 9,450,000 square miles (24,474,000 sq km).

North America has many kinds of land. There are dry deserts, cold tundra, and rain forests. This continent also has beautiful mountains and lakes. The natural beauty of North America makes it a special place.

Where Is North America?

The equator is an imaginary line. It divides the earth into two halves. The top half is the Northern Hemisphere. North America is in the Northern Hemisphere.

West of North America is the Pacific Ocean. The Atlantic Ocean is east of North America. The Arctic Ocean lies north of North America.

A narrow strip of land joins North America to South America. This piece of land is called an isthmus.

Greenland is an island in the Atlantic Ocean. It is also part of North America.

Arctic
Ocean

Greenland

NORTH AMERICA

Pacific Ocean

Atlantic Ocean

Isthmus of Panama

Equator

SOUTH AMERICA

Countries

There are 23 countries in North America. Canada is the biggest North American country. The country with the most people is the United States. Most people in Canada and the United States speak English.

Thirteen countries are on islands in the Caribbean Sea. Together, these islands are called the West Indies. Spanish is a common language there.

Spanish is common in Mexico and Central America, too. Seven countries make up Central America. They are on the south end of North America's mainland.

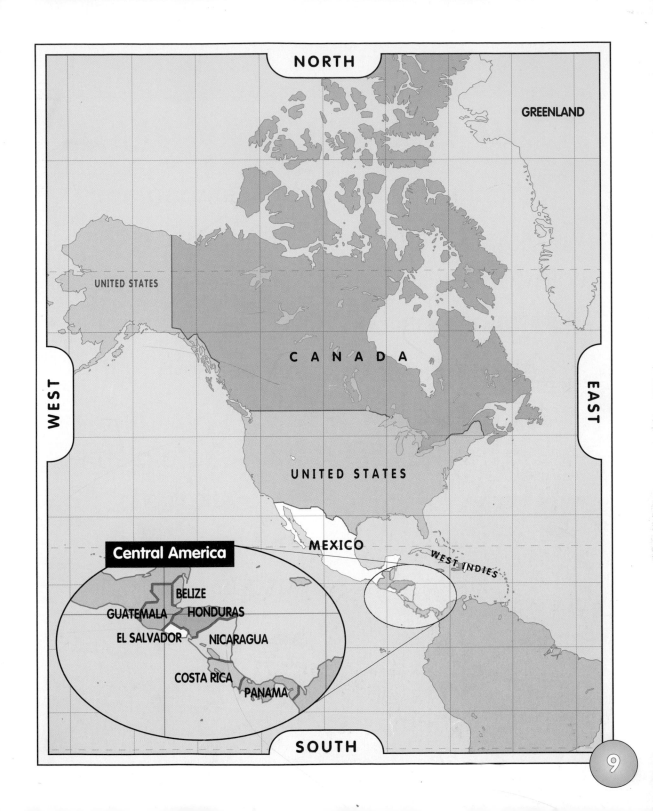

Cold Tundra

Greenland and parts of Canada and Alaska are in the Arctic. The Arctic is the cold area around the North Pole. Arctic winters are long and very cold.

The ground stays mostly frozen in the Arctic. This land is called tundra. The tundra has no trees. Some tundra plants are arctic moss, bearberry, and pasque flowers.

A polar bear among bearberry plants.

Seals (left) and walruses (right) live
in the cold Arctic.

Many animals can live in the Arctic.
A few of them are polar bears, seals,
and walruses.

Few people besides the Inuit live in this
cold land. The Inuit lived in Canada and
Alaska before anyone else.

A polar bear

An Inuit child

Greenland

Greenland's true name is Kalaallit Nunaat. It is the biggest island in the world. Ice covers most of this island. Only about 55,000 people live there. Most of these people live on Greenland's coast.

Many Inuit people live in Greenland.

Dry Deserts

Deserts are very dry places. Deserts get less than 10 inches (25 cm) of rain each year. There are deserts in southwestern United States and in Mexico. There are four main desert areas:

- Great Basin
- Sonoran
- Mojave
- Chihuahuan

The Sonoran Desert

The Mojave is the smallest North American desert. The Mojave is the driest, too. It can get very hot in the Mojave Desert. But not all deserts are hot. The Great Basin Desert is a cold desert. It snows there.

The Mojave Desert

Cactus

Armadillo

Joshua trees, cacti, and wildflowers grow in North America's deserts. Bighorn sheep, coyotes, snakes, scorpions, armadillos, and tortoises live there, too. Tortoises are turtles that live on land.

Tropical Places

Rain forests get over 80 inches (2 m) of rain each year. These forests are warm and wet, or tropical. Central America has many tropical rain forests.

A North American rain forest

Sloths live in rain forests.

Many kinds of animals live in Central America's rain forests. There are monkeys, quetzals, and sloths. Quetzals are green and red birds. They eat avocados and other fruits. Sloths are slow-moving animals. They hang upside down in trees and eat leaves and fruit.

A tropical swamp in Florida

Another tropical place is the Florida Everglades. It is a big, swampy grassland in southeastern United States. Alligators, bobcats, pelicans, and many other animals live there.

Alligators (above) and pelicans (below)
live in the Florida Everglades.

Tall Mountains

Rocky Mountains

Western North America has many mountain ranges. These mountains stretch from Alaska to Central America. Twenty mountain ranges make up the Rocky Mountains. The Rocky Mountains are about 3,000 miles (4,800 km) long.

Mount McKinley is a mountain of the Alaska Range. It is in Alaska. The top of Mount McKinley is the highest point in North America. It is 20,320 feet (6,194 m) high. Denali is another name for Mount McKinley. It means the Great One.

Mount McKinley

The oldest mountains in North America are the Appalachians. These mountains are about half as tall as the Rocky Mountains. They are in eastern North America. The Appalachians begin in Canada and end in Alabama. Alabama is in the United States's southeast.

The Appalachian Mountains

America's Breadbasket

Flat lands are called plains. The plains of the United States are good for farming. Some people call this land America's Breadbasket. Farmers grow wheat, corn, soybeans, and other crops. People also raise cattle and sheep on the plains.

Great Lakes

Lake Superior is the biggest freshwater lake in the world. It is one of the five Great Lakes in North America. The other four Great Lakes are:

- Lake Erie
- Lake Huron
- Lake Michigan
- Lake Ontario

Ships can sail from the Great Lakes to the Atlantic Ocean. These ships bring goods to other parts of the world.

There are about 35,000 islands in the Great Lakes.

Chicago is a city on Lake Michigan.

Visiting North America

The Grand Canyon is in the United States. It is in the southwestern state of Arizona.

A canyon is a deep valley. The Grand Canyon is one mile (1,609 m) deep. It is 18 miles (29 km) wide and 275 miles (443 km) long. At the bottom of the canyon is the Colorado River.

Many people visit the Grand Canyon each year. They enjoy the wilderness in and around the canyon. The Grand Canyon is a beautiful part of North America.

The Grand Canyon

North America

- North America is the third-largest **continent**.

- Mount McKinley is the highest point in North America.

- More than 400 million people live in North America.

- Lake Superior is the largest North American lake.

- Canada is the largest country in North America.

- North America's lowest point is in Death Valley, California.

- North America's Grand Canyon is the biggest canyon in the world.

Important Words

continent one of the earth's seven main land areas.

equator an imaginary line around the earth. It divides the earth into two halves.

island land that has water on all sides.

isthmus a narrow strip of land that joins two larger land areas.

mainland the main part of a continent.

tropical weather that is warm and wet.

tundra flat land with no trees in the far north.

Web Sites

Would you like to learn more about North America?
Please visit ABDO Publishing Company on the World Wide Web to find web site links about North America. These links are routinely monitored and updated to provide the most current information available.

www.abdopub.com

Index